MARSHMALLOW CLOUDS

Two Poets at Play among Figures of Speech

Ted Kooser and Connie Wanek

illustrated by Richard Jones

CANDLEWICK PRESS

For Zachary, Lily, and Marilynn
TK

To Julia and Isaac Baxter
CW

For Desnee
RJ

A DISAPPOINTMENT

I thought I saw a winter tree
clowning around on the top of a hill,
up on one leg and juggling a pie

on the end of a stick, but my friend
who always sees things as they are
told me no, that both the clown

and the pie were all in my
imagination; that what was really
there was only a squirrel nest

out on the end of a branch,
and the nest was old and cold,
and even the squirrel was gone.

FIRE

METEOR SHOWER

Just before sunrise
I counted nine meteors
scratching the heavens,
just little scratches,
the kind a cat might make
while playing with a ball,
a great black cat
and an enormous ball
that glittered, everything
and all of us inside.

THUNDERSTORM

This one's gotten up in the night
and, not wanting to wake us,
stumbles around, bumping the walls
of the long empty hallway leading away,
now and then lighting a match
and then, just as quickly, blowing it out.

JULY

One summer day I was boiled and salted
like a peanut. I was the meat
in a heat sandwich, the dog in a hot.
I was the crimson crayon
melting in a sunny car,
the color of firecrackers and flags
and Mars, where once water
cooled the red stones.

Finally the sun set
and someone let the crickets out,
then opened the firefly jar.
The darkness filled with blinking stars
like whispers for my eyes.

A SECRET

It's safe to tell a secret to the stars,
aliens all. They haven't
a word of English,
which means they are reliable
in their silence.

If you write a secret down
and send it up,
the stars will burn it.
The fire that they are is meant
for such chores.

It's good to free a secret
and let the place in your chest
where it clawed you like a badger
scar over and heal.

The badger means no harm.
All secrets hate to feel trapped.
When they see the slightest sliver
of light, they take flight
to the nearest star.

GAS

Sometimes gas is a liquid
that can burn.
If you're careful
you never smell it on your hands.
It's a first cousin, perhaps,
of fat, that doesn't mix with water,
related also to pine pitch,
the golden blood of the tree.

I look at the big oaks
and imagine them after another
million years, filling
someone's gas tank with acorns.

But so much happens over
immense amounts of time, such as
365 horses turning into an engine,
and someday, if we're lucky,
back into horses.

IN NOVEMBER

The leaves at the tops of the trees
are the last to fall. They cling
to summer as the first cold winds
begin to pinch at them like
someone's fingers trying to put out
the flames of a thousand candles,
and for each extinguished there are
two more burning, and another,
over there.

FIREPLACE

We keep our fire safe in a playpen
where we feed it,
mostly leftovers from the woods,
and fire is a good eater,
tasting everything.
It can grow quickly, gnawing on
each new log. Then
like a happy wolf pup, it howls.
It has no stomach, though. So fire
is never full, never satisfied.
That's why, no matter how it begs,
we must never set it free.

WATER

BOAT

An aluminum boat has been left upside down
up on blocks at the edge of the water.
It looks like a hand cupped over a shadow
to keep it from scuttling away. There's just
enough air for the shadow to breathe
and it's pulled in its head and its bleached
wooden oars and is waiting. It's been waiting
all summer, and maybe for thousands of years,
peering out at the meddlesome world.

SPRING

A wake of black waves foamy with pebbles
follows the plow, rolls all the way up
to the fence, slaps into the grass and trickles
back, while farther out a spray of white gulls
splashes down. Spring on the prairie,
a sunny day, a sky reaching out to forever
in every direction, and here at my feet,
distilled from all that blue, a single drop
caught in the spoon of a leaf, a robin's egg.

THE WORLD WITHOUT ME

I took a walk after the rain.
Another world was in each puddle,
shimmering, clouds racing,
trees upside down.

My world—ours—never really cared,
which didn't seem quite fair.
The ocean should be sorry
when it drowns a person.

Then I saw a worm
in a puddle, still alive,
gesturing to me. The worm
was visible in two worlds,

above and below, its white-pink
body swelling from water. I don't know
if it was in pain—maybe—and though
I didn't want to touch it,

I reached down and snatched it up
and laid it in the low grass.
In the world without me, the worm died.
But in this world, I saved a worm.

TADPOLE

Why think frog?
Why not enjoy the tadpole
just as it appears, a huge comma,
soft and black. It doesn't
smear in a water droplet,
so maybe it's been shaped
with a dull Sharpie, permanent ink,
perhaps by someone just learning
to draw, someone who has to try
another and another
until the golden pool is full
of swimming tadpoles,
the liveliest of all punctuation.

WHY PETS DON'T WRITE

Parrots could, actually,
but they don't believe that's
any of your business.

Dogs don't have time to write.
Cats do, but they say things like
"Guess what I think? You never will."

A horse is a poem
galloping in the windy pasture,
a poem that says,
"Saddle me and I'll still be free."

Guppies hide their tiny pages underwater,
down in the gravel. You'll need
to hold your breath to read
"I'm hungry" and "I'm always afraid."

SLEEP

Each hour of sleep is an hour of healing.
The body straightens, the shoulders
settle, the wrists wilt, the fists
open like yellow water lilies.

Some of us can hardly wait to sleep
and grow taller. Others don't trust
themselves to the night, no matter
that the stars have never

done them any harm, nor the owl
in the oak tree. For some it's as though
dreams won't let them go. They are afraid
to climb on this silent raft of moonlight.

AIR

BARRED OWL

He takes whichever seat is available
at the back of the dawn and settles in,
pulling his old gray overcoat around him,
and now and then throughout the morning
he hoots, but softly, like a man calling out
from a dream. None of us could find him
if we looked, but if we hoot correctly
sometimes he'll come, soundless, tree to tree
like somebody shuffling along in his slippers,
eyes burning, peevish for being disturbed,
his claws curled back and hidden in his sleeves.

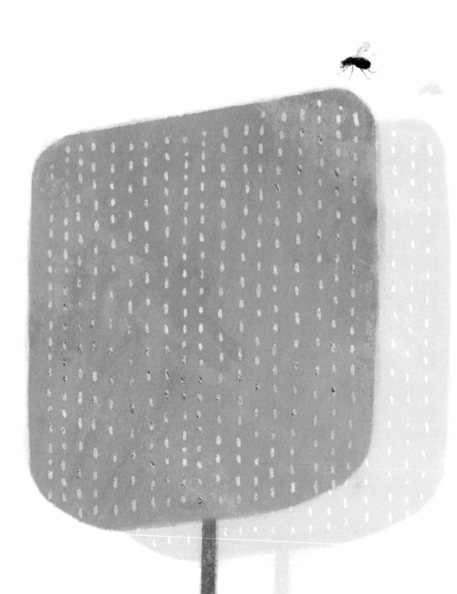

FLYSWATTER

The handle's like an old wire hanger,
the kind that tangles with its neighbors.

The business end is plastic,
made in China for Chinese flies

which are similar enough to ours
that this tool requires

no physical translation.
Fly's an active verb, present tense,

always present, always tense.
A swing and a miss, strike two,

then a fly to center field
and a mess on the window glass.

Sometimes a fly will even land
right on the swatter, bold as a spy.

JUNE AFTERNOON

The sky is all covered with cobwebs,
wisps of them, drifting so high
that probably no one could reach them
with a rag on a broom, and not a soul
is trying. How did it come to this?
Hundreds of people with time on their hands
and not one broom in the air!

MARSHMALLOWS

A marshmallow feels soft
and lightly powdered
like a grandmother's cheek.
A full bag is like a pillow
filled with little pillows.

Once I put a few white marshmallows
on a big blue plate and thought,
They're partly cloudy!

Most find marshmallows too
sweet, too sticky inside,
like the edge of a Post-it note
where someone wrote,
Don't bother!

HARPIST

She has taken a great golden moth
into her arms, and with both hands
she keeps its wings pressed closed
to keep it from flying away.
And now she is drawing it closer
and smoothing the veins in its wings
as if to comfort it or give it pleasure,
and the dust that she brushes away
sprinkles into the circle of light,
tinkling as if it were music.

REMOTE

The TV remote means
to change the world
one channel at a time.

It's designed for the human hand
the way a pacifier fits exactly
where a baby cries.

You think it's yours, but no:
the remote and the TV screen
work only as a pair.

Your fingertip is essential, though,
just as Aladdin's warm palm
summoned the genie of the lamp:

"Your wish is my command!"
What, master, will it please you
to watch? says the remote.

But if you know
which button to press, you can
mute all this babbling.

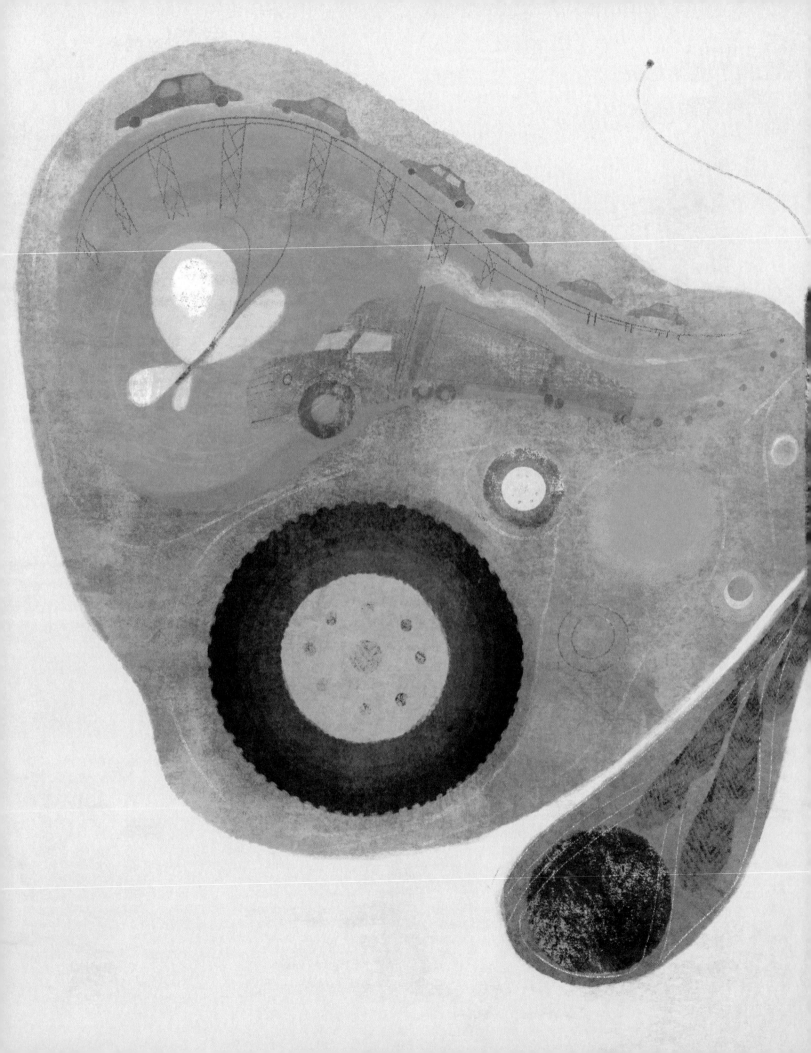

BUTTERFLY LUCK

A few feet over a busy highway,
as if caught in a box of glass,
a pale yellow butterfly flutters,
desperately trying the sides,

trying the corners, as a semi
with grasshoppers pasted all over
its teeth roars toward it. But
a heap of hot wind, pushed in front

of the truck, gets under the box
and lofts it high in the air,
where it rolls over and over,
bouncing along on its corners

the full length of the trailer,
then bounds off the back
with the butterfly flying inside.
That's butterfly luck.

EARTH

WINTER PONIES

Out in the frozen pasture
three ponies turn their rumps
to the wind. Their winter hair
has come in thick
and dull as a muskrat's,
a sure sign of hard times to come.
We'll never get close enough
to see the frost on their eyelashes,
like white mascara,
or lay a hand on their long forelocks.
They're stubborn, and know
only one master, the snow.

BOOK

Oh, sandwich delicious, my book!
The folded pita of your covers,
a layer of mayo your table of contents,
a few words of mustard introducing
the chewy salami of history, complete
with its peppercorn footnotes,
and then there's the ripe, stinky cheese
of your author's conclusions!
Setting you down on my table,
I slip my crisp bookmark inside you,
a leaf of romaine!

A BAD DREAM

Deep in the night, a frightening dream
tried my door, and I called out for help,
my voice all alone in the silence.
The moon showed up almost at once,
wearing its white latex gloves, and dusted
the doorknob for prints and checked all
the windows for damage. After a while
I was able to go back to sleep, and by dawn
I felt better, and swept open the curtains,
and the sun was out there, keeping watch,
and ribbons of light like crime-scene tape
stretched from the trees at the edge
of my property all the way up to my door.

THE VILLAGE TENNIS COURT

The old net was a sagging obstacle
till one day it fell altogether,
and nothing stood between us.

The court was an open road now,
lines painted down the middle and on
each side, and the ball was traffic, one car

rolling to a stop with a flat tire.
We never kept score; you never had to
crush me and I never had to cheat.

Grass grew in every crooked crack,
impossible to pull. If you tugged,
it broke off in your hand like a lizard's tail.

This grass was the prairie coming
back to life, mowing down all lofty
human notions, blade by blade.

BARN

This old barn doesn't know where it is
because it has never been anywhere else,
but what's it missed? The city, come on,
all those two-stall and three-stall garages
elbow to elbow all along the streets?
No way. It likes what it has, its peace
and quiet, the things it's collected, buckets
of bent nails one day to be straightened,
a tractor that hasn't been started for years,
the softening cardboard cartons of parts
for machinery it scarcely remembers.
Day in and day out it wakes and pulls on
its patched-up underwear of rotten boards
beneath its coveralls of corrugated metal,
and looks out over what's always the same,
and combs its roof straight down the middle.

COW PIE

People who live in cities
never get to accidentally step
in a cow pie. You never find them
fresh, steaming on a concrete street
near a parking meter
in front of the French bakery.
No one puts alfalfa in a pie
the way a cow does.

TREES

Trees are born blind and in need of each other.
With luck they come up in a forest with brothers
and sisters to listen to. Growing up for a tree
is mostly reaching out and out to touch another,
and that's enough of a life. None of them know
where they are, but that's OK. It doesn't matter.
They don't ask for much, a good rain now and then,
and what they like most are the sweet smells
of the others, and the warm touch of the light,
and to join the soft singing that goes on and on.

AFTERWORD

From Ted:

Each of us is born with the gift of an imagination and, as if it were a favorite cat or dog, playing with your imagination can keep it healthy and happy. The poems in this book are about fooling around, about letting one's imagination run free with whatever it comes upon. Our idea is to encourage you to run with your own imagination, to enjoy what you come up with.

Here's a picture of me as a boy, letting my imagination turn an everyday soda bottle into a submarine.

SUBMARINE

Using a corked pop bottle weighted with sand,
trying again and again to get the weight right
so the bottle would float at a steady level
just a few inches under the surface, invisible
under a sea I'd filled my mother's washtub with,
I spent hours and hours, but my submarine
would either very slowly sink or very slowly
float to the surface, water streaming away
from its hull, vulnerable to any destroyer
that might come steaming down, alarm blaring,
out of the shadowy coal room next to the furnace,
and day after day I was hopelessly sealed
in damp submarine air, in a small circle of light
from an overhead bulb, already a captain at ten,
alone with my dream and a bottle of sand.

And here's Connie:

What Ted says is true. Sometimes trees or clouds or horses or other people—or even a certain car or the gas that runs it—seem to summon our imaginations. For me, and maybe for you, it's fun to listen for voices from unexpected places. The refrigerator at our house just now turned on, and I thought I heard a crabby grumble, because it was up quite a bit last night, working hard to keep the food cool, as all of us slept in peace. Machines can be such complainers!

Anyway, here's a look at a turtle, and what my imagination felt he might be up to.

TURTLE

The turtle never married.
Every day he swam
laps around the lake
to clean his house.
Sometimes he heard
a knock on his shell,
but "Do come in"
he never said.

The turtle was very
attached to where he lived
and never wandered far.
His shell was the shape
of a tiny old car
with turtle feet for wheels,
a tail instead of a trunk,

and zero room for
nosy passengers.

First edition 2022

Library of Congress Catalog Card Number 2021947131
ISBN 978-1-5362-0303-5

23 24 25 26 APS 10 9 8 7 6 5 4 3

Printed in Humen, Dongguan, China

This book was typeset in ITC Esprit.
The illustrations were rendered in paint and edited digitally.

Candlewick Press
99 Dover Street
Somerville, Massachusetts 02144

www.candlewick.com